Table of Contents

A Magical Place

Leaves of all colors and shapes
crackle under your feet as you walk.
The crisp, blue sky peeks through
a blanket of branches above you.
Woodland animals scurry to their
nests and dens.

No wonder so many fairy tale characters live in the forest! The forest is a magical place.

What Are Forests?

Forests are large areas of land covered with many trees and other plant life. In the forest, tall trees rise above plants that grow much closer to the forest floor.

Small forests are also known as woods.

Did you know that there is more than one kind of forest?

Some forests have trees whose leaves change color in the **autumn**. By winter, most leaves fall to the ground. Then the trees rest until new leaves grow in the spring.

In other forests, **evergreen** trees grow. The leaves of most evergreen trees do not change color or fall away. These trees stay green all year long.

Trees that grow needles need less water than trees that grow other kinds of leaves.

Some evergreen trees have **needles** for leaves. They may also grow **cones**.

One pine tree in California is the oldest living thing on Earth. It is over 4,800 years old!

Cones have seeds inside them to grow new trees. But watch out! Squirrels like to eat the seeds before they have a chance to grow.

Another kind of forest is called a **rainforest**. As you can guess, a rainforest gets a lot of water. Trees and plants there are very green and moist.

But not all rainforests get a lot of rain. Sometimes they get a lot of fog and moist air instead. The fog brings the water they need to help the trees grow.

Where Are They?

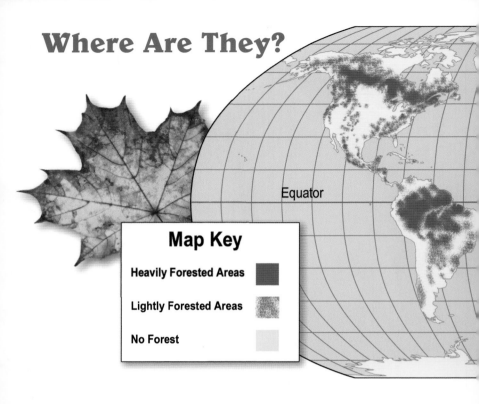

Equator

Map Key

Heavily Forested Areas

Lightly Forested Areas

No Forest

Forests can be found all over the world, but the kind of forest depends on where it is.

Forests that change color are found in many places, but mainly in the eastern United States, Canada, Europe, Russia, China, and Japan.

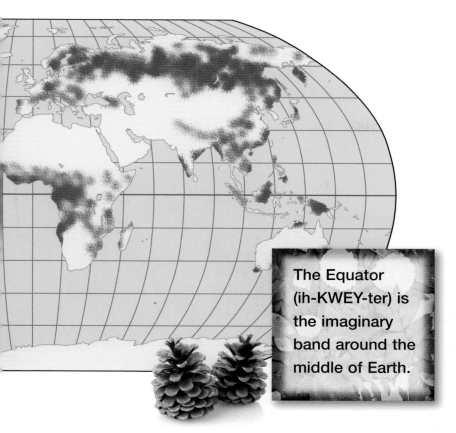

The Equator (ih-KWEY-ter) is the imaginary band around the middle of Earth.

Forests filled with cone and needle trees are only in the north.

Many rainforests are near the Equator. Other rainforests are near coasts, mainly in the northwestern United States.

Animals in the Forest

Different kinds of forests have different kinds of animals, too.

red fox

raccoon

skunk

turkey

black bear

deer

In forests where the leaves change color and fall, you might see raccoons and squirrels hunting for nuts. You might see deer in a clearing or black bears peeking around trees. Foxes, turkeys, skunks, and rabbits may be nearby.

During the winter, these forests are much quieter. Many animals hibernate or go to warmer places when it gets cold.

hibernating dormouse

wolf

Great Grey owl

bobcat

In the evergreen forests where needles and cones grow on trees, moose and wolves roam the land. Beavers build their dams, and

moose

beaver

Great Grey owls hoot from the trees. If you look quickly, you might see a bobcat running beneath the branches.

ring-tailed lemur

spider monkey

rainbow lorikeet

Animals live in rainforests, too. In fact, there are so many animals that the rainforest can be a very noisy place! Monkeys chatter as they swing from vines. Colorful

How many plants and animals are in the rainforests? There are millions of species!

tree frog

birds call to each other from the trees and sky. Bright green, red, and orange frogs croak as they hop along the ground.

poison dart frogs

Dangers to the Forest

Forests are an important part
of our world, but many things are
a danger to them. Fires sometimes
burn down forests as far as you can
see. Insects and sickness can spread